It's Not about You: One man's journey through his life to truly understand the meaning of leadership in its truest form.

`I0486027`

This book is dedicated to my family without which I would have been gone long ago. To My wife, Janet, of thirty years...how have you put up with me for so long? I am continually mystified yet eternally grateful for your love and support. To our children, Andrew, Thomas and Matthew you are and continue to be the light of your mother's and my lives! Realize your passion to do whatever you want to do and learn to be happy...if there is one thing I would tell you is to learn how to be happy.

Forward By:

Michael Owens

C.E.O. of Dewolff, Boberg & Associates

I like winning! It gave me great pleasure and self-worth to know that I made things happen. I enjoyed the glory of accomplishments and expected the due rewards that normally accompanied with achieving targets. My job was to personally train and develop my clients as a consultant. When my bosses came to visit my projects, I paraded them in front of my clients, and I orchestrated meetings where my clients would heap praises upon praises on my abilities to help them get better. I knew that these actions would also convert into me getting more rewards for my hard work and achievements. Life was good. I liked being the best. When my peers became envious of my relationship with upper management, I rationalized that it was a part of "survival of the fittest." I felt that I had all the answers. As long as my bosses were happy, my projects were doing well, and I was able to generate more business then these indicators showed that I was on a good path. Life couldn't get any better. I loved my life as an individual contributor! I was only responsible for myself. Unfortunately, this life existed for only six months! I was asked to be a Project Manager because I was such a good individual contributor. I was all of 23 years old.

My path into management began early but not all that unusual. Many people are picked to be in management positions because they are and were good individual contributors. Many companies promote people based on accomplishments, skills, smarts or seniority. Pathways into management can vary widely, such as major corporations recruiting the best of the best from top colleges and running them through a management-training loop. Many times the best are the ones who are the smartest and most driven. Somewhere along the way as they receive greater responsibility, their controlling nature or the fear of failure will reveal itself and sabotage them. As the old saying goes, "Right next to our greatest strength lies our greatest weakness."

Once I became a manager, I worked harder and longer. I did not want to fail and I certainly did not want to disappoint my management. As hard as I was working, I expected my people to work just as hard. I felt that I needed to whip them in shape. I had all the answers. All they had to do was listen to me. All they had to do was follow my directions. All they had to do was exactly what I was doing. Was that too much to ask? In the end, they all disappointed me. I had to step in and do their jobs on top of my job. Things became better, but I was getting resentful of my people because they couldn't see that I was pulling their weight. Instead of being grateful, I felt that they didn't respect me enough, trust me enough, or emulate me enough. They were all older than me so I reasoned that it must have to do with their work ethic. The entire problem was with them. All I needed was better people who had better work ethics and could follow basic instructions.

A year later, I was leading this same team on another assignment, which was even more difficult. Halfway into the project, every member on my team quit! I was left alone to do all the work myself. I had to continue the project with a brand new team. I knew at this point that something had to change. I knew the change had to start with me. I was 27 years old.

The topic of management and leadership has been around for a long time. Often times, a successful business leader or a coach will produce a book following a successful event such as a turnaround of a company or a winning season. I still remember a book by a CEO who believed in cutting cost as the best way to manage a corporation and he came out with a management book called "Chain Saw Al." Sometimes, we view good management or good leadership based on outcome or results. We don't always get to read the heart and soul of the management philosophy that may have influenced the people who were responsible for the outcome. Rather, we get perspectives on business strategies, timing of the market or a relationship with a good player who learned to be a great player to lead a team to a championship.

In Doug's book, I found a refreshing perspective on management shared from a very personal place. Doug's view of management is more about his own personal journey rather than a series of prescriptive ideas on how we can become better managers. The "golden nuggets" are less about building a better "mouse-trap" and more about Doug's lessons learned through his personal and profession mistakes made over his lifetime. His humility translated into candor is where the real lessons can be gained.

When Doug reached out to me to be his mentor, I was really caught off guard. I've known Doug for a long time but we never really crossed paths. Once Doug was promoted to the Chief of Operations, I would see Doug in our internal monthly meetings and on occasion, I would run into Doug in meeting with our clients. Majority of these encounters would result in Doug and I interacting passively since I usually worked closer with Doug's boss, so Doug reaching out to me came as a complete surprise.

In addition to Doug asking me to be his mentor being a surprise was that his request was a first for me since I was never asked to be a mentor by anyone. I do have many direct reports whom I groom, train and develop and I make it a habit of talking to many of these folks on a daily basis, where I focus on their personal development, but to be a mentor for a person whom I did not know very well and who reported to my direct report was uncharted waters! After the initial shock, I tried to let Doug down gently since I already had over ten direct reports and I really didn't think I had the time. After further discussion with Doug, I realized that reaching out to me was not easy for him and his sincerity came through with flying colors. I apologized for my initial reaction and we agreed to a weekly phone call to start our mentoring sessions.

Our weekly calls have lasted over two years. Every week, we get on the phone for an hour. We talk about many topics and over time it has matured. Our topics included personal, personnel and often about the role of management within DBA.

On many instances, I would wrap up our weekly call by telling Doug that I often feel like the student because I learned so much from our weekly calls.

Over past several years, our company was and still is going through a transformation. Our company provides a management consulting service where we help our clients drive accountability at the front line management level. Since our consultants leave their homes on Sunday nights and they don't get home till Friday nights, we ask a lot of our people and they truly sacrifice their personal time for their noble profession. It is a difficult job and since the project duration is six months long, many of our consultants get new bosses and work with new project members at least three times a year. Based on the nature of the beast, people in management must learn to be consistent in the way they manage people so that the stress level of working for a new boss and developing a working relationship with new members do not become overwhelming for our consultants. Based on this challenge, DBA is going through a transformation where good management practices are analyzed, reviewed and audited to ensure best management possible for our people to grow and to flourish.

During the transformation, the changes have been tough for our people and since I was the one initiating these changes, I knew that many of our people in management were personally struggling with this challenge. This is where Doug played a critical role because he was in the trenches with our people and his peers. Doug took it on himself to talk with many of his peers and was able to give first-hand knowledge of frustrations and fears that the people in Project Management was going through. On our weekly calls, Doug was able to give me some critical insights and we had open discussions about the personal challenges that our people were going through. This feedback was absolutely paramount for me to vary my speed, communication, changes in direction of the transformation. Doug and I realized that in order to drive ownership and accountability at the Project Management level, who owned the consultants the company's biggest challenges were the Chief of Operations whom the PM's reported to. These weekly calls were personal and I often found myself learning through Doug's perspective and after a while the mentor became the student.

In this book, I have found many of our discussion that were to be useful for me as a leader. Putting our people first is not a slogan but a series of actions and only way to determine whether you as a leader are being as effective as you can be is through how your people view you as a leader and their view of the organization. Earning the right credibility with the people you are trying to lead comes to mind. Whether as a leader you are being honest with yourself to view yourself through your people is a very difficult thing and it does take a lot of personal courage, but once you've acquired this skill, it is immensely gratifying. Through Doug's help, I am getting better at it but still have a lot to learn.

It's Not About You!

1 THE BEGINNING

In the past thirty plus years of my adult life I must admit that I have not always been what one would call an "active participant". By this I mean that I may have been an observer but did not always take control of my direction or desired outcome. Today there is much about "GenXers" and "Millennial's" and how their value systems are significantly different than those of us "Baby Boomers". I could not disagree enough with these generalizations! When I was in my late twenties and early thirties I felt that I was "owed" promotions, salary increases etc... didn't you people know who I am?? Not much different than my adult children feel today so do I see a need to handle their needs differently...no I do not, a clear understanding of a few facts will typically set people's perspectives.

1. Life is not always fair...nobody told you it would be!
2. Ultimately you are compensated for the value that you bring...period.
3. Hard work is its own reward.
4. The easy way is always the wrong way!

These simple truths continue to be proven out, even in today's ultra-entitled driven society. In the past 3 to 5 years I have come to the conclusion that my life to date has been a farce...I have been a self-absorbed, self-centered person for many years and there are many, many examples I can give but it will suffice to say that there are enough people out there to testify to these facts. Over these past several years I have received personal attention, coaching and mentoring that has allowed me to see past the "Me" in most things. Understanding, whether it be as a father, husband, friend, employee or leader that nothing I do can or should be about me has been the most difficult yet rewarding journey I have ever undertaken. Most of us intellectually understand the idea, many understand conceptually why the idea is correct, but very few actually enact the changes necessary in their lives, actions, communication, and focus to really demonstrate this altered state to those around us. This simple truth has taken me an entire life to get to, and embracing this concept completely has given me much peace and contentment here late in my life.

I have an incredible wife of over thirty years that has put up with my nonsense while on this journey, our three boys have turned out to be solid citizens and are developing into good men, husbands and they will be great fathers when that time comes. I think that everyone reading this has a similar claim, but in my case I can tell you that these things that I am most thankful for and blessed with I did not earn through my actions these were gifts afforded me by a gracious God. If I truly got what I have sowed over these many years my life would be incredibly sad and lonely.

It's Not About You is my attempt to put into words my enlightenment and journey to this current point in my life. I have by no means "Arrived" and I struggle with this most basic of concepts daily, but my heart is right which assists me with the focus necessary to continue down the path. Hopefully this will assist, in a small way, in your journey and if this can have any impact on just one person then my efforts are well worth it.

2 LEADERSHIP

There are entire libraries written about this subject and I will not try to summarize in any way all of the varied attempts of defining this intangible ability. What I will do is try to convey how I have come to define Leadership.

Leadership: *Is evidenced through an individual or organization's actions, characteristics and communication that is singularly focused on the care and growth of others, either in their sphere of influence or organization. Effective leadership is demonstrated through the development of others to assume additional responsibilities and successfully create outcomes that are consistent with either their personal goals or an organizational goals and or needs.*

Basically what I am trying to say here is that there is a need to understand that as a spouse, parent, friend, employee, manager, Vice President or CEO you are in a position to influence others and design outcomes. If you are not completely focused on the positive outcomes for those within your network then the leadership function become more of a technical exercise rather than a personal investment in the success of others. We have all seen the first form of leadership...I did it this way for many years! I did not want to invest in others because I knew that at some point in time I was going to be disappointed and or have to have disciplinary conversations that were going to not be very fun to have. I felt that if I used the "Captain Of The Ship" model then I would not be vulnerable and I could compartmentalize the experiences and thus stay out of the emotion. When doing this it was very easy for me to justify the mistreatment of those around me...to include my family. I was demeaning, rude, mean, inflexible etc... all of which has been demonstrated to me from the fact that I have difficulty pointing out those that I have influenced to be greater people. If you can understand that great leaders beget more great leaders then the way you measure success as a leader is in how many people have you influenced, positively, to take on more responsibility and stand up for what they believe in? In my case I have difficulty doing this...I am trying to make up for lost time in this but I am starting this effort far too late in my life.

Leaders inspire others to greater efforts through how they live their lives and in how they treat others along the way. It is not about always being the "nice" person, it's about personally investing in others emotionally to assist them with setting the right goals or expectations and then holding them and yourself accountable to achieving the expectations or exceeding them. Sometimes these discussions are uncomfortable for both parties as you are emotionally investing in this other person's success or lack thereof and due to this investment, you feel the elation of success and the pain of failure as keenly as the person you are investing in.

3 SUCCESS

One of the most important items to think through is how YOU define success...not how the world views success but how do you as a person, spouse, parent, employee, or leader define success. I can attest to the fact that this is not an exercise in academics but this is an intensely personal activity that must be discussed with those around you that are the most important in your life. For me this was over thirty years in the making!

1. Am I taking care of my responsibilities as a husband and father in a way that is nurturing and helpful? Yes, financial stability is part of this equation but being that dad that loves his wife and kids and is not afraid to show it is something that was never really demonstrated to me with my parents and thus I have done a very poor job at demonstrating this to my wife and children...this is very important to me, I must make this change in my life in order to have a positive influence on my kids and their kid's lives after I am dead and gone.

2. Influencing those around me at work in a positive way. Am I creating a sphere of influence that is assisting others in achieving their goals, both personally and professionally? Am I emotionally investing in the right way? Am I opening myself up to those development conversations that although emotionally draining, yield great results in the other person's life? Am I putting others first in my thoughts and activities or am I still being selfish in nature?

3. Patience!! I am continually working on being patient...being quiet inside and listening to those around me is not a strength that I readily possess. Accepting what I cannot influence or change while working on those items that I can is another way to look at this, again if you have an elevated viewpoint of your abilities and worth you will struggle with this.

4. Love Life!! I am truly a blessed man...how do I show this to those around me? I have a wonderful and supportive family both at home and at work! I love my professional life much as I do my personal life...how fortunate can one be? Do I show this in my demeanor and communications on a daily basis?

4 SACRIFICE

I personally do not believe that leaders are born to it, I believe that great leaders are built...through life experiences, and examples, I feel that a person is influenced to greatness...or not. Due to this I also believe that personal sacrifice is part of the equation that plays into an individual's ability to inspire others. Sacrifice can take many forms in life, if you look at someone like Martin Luther King, he sacrificed his own safety and comfort for what he believed to be right and true...he stood up to be counted full well understanding that the most likely conclusion was going to be ridicule, exclusion from the mainstream of life at that time and possibly physical harm to him and potentially members of his family. How many examples of this willingness to sacrifice to we see today? Not many, one of the most shining examples that I hold onto is that of a gentleman named Rick Rescorla. Rick served in the US Army during Vietnam and participated in many pitched and hard fought battles such as the fight at LZ X-ray and LZ Albany. Rick proved over and over again that he was not only one to be counted on when the fighting was hand to hand but marvelously inspirational in the songs that he would sing while on the front lines to calm his troopers. Rick demonstrated these leadership characteristics again on September 11th 2001 while directing the evacuation of those in his charge from the South Tower. After the first plane hit the North Tower the security personnel told those in the South Tower to stay put, Rick's response was "Bugger That!!" and he proceeded to cajole, prod and downright order people out of the tower. Over 2,000 people were trekking down from high floors while the drama unfolded outside, to calm these traders, bankers, and financial planners Rick sang the same Cornish battle hymns he used on those far flung battlefields in Vietnam. How many people can say they were instrumental in saving over 2,000 Mom's, Dad's, Sons and Daughters?? Rick died in the collapse of the south tower because he went back into the tower to make sure that he got all of those he could...it was never about Rick, it was ALWAYS about others!! Most of us cannot have such dramatic stories as these, but we do have our own experiences and we can make cognitive decisions to put others first in all that we do. That to me is a form of servant leadership that can only be defined as a sacrifice, thoughtfully putting others wellbeing, development and success at the forefront of our efforts is noble in nature and in the end generates its own rewards. One tenet of leadership that continually rings true through the years is the fact that if you feel that serving others is beneath you then the ability to inspire and lead others is beyond you...period.

5 HUMILITY

Humility is hard to take or demonstrate at times, accepting feedback on weaknesses without making justifications for the shortcomings is not something that comes naturally to most people...especially those in a leadership position. Learning how to accept the feedback from people that may be technically subordinate to you within an org chart is not something that we are taught in a school of business. That characteristic is developed over time through effective coaching and mentoring which will ultimately, down the road, lead to getting your heart right and synched up with your thoughts that manifest themselves through your actions...every day! Many of us are very adept at pretending to be humble, however although we put that face on at work many times at home we are anything but humble...or at least that is my story. I was the best at what I did and was not afraid to tell my family this in very forceful terms...who was I trying to convince, them or me? Humility is something that is demonstrated by others that you see as influential in your life and due to this you desire to emulate the same characteristic. If this is not demonstrated to you by your parents, grandparents, teachers, coaches etc... then you will struggle with this simple principal as you step into a leadership position either as a spouse/parent or as a manager at your job.

Humility is not something that we see demonstrated by many in leadership positions whether it be politically, business or sports. We see people that are self-absorbed with what THEY did...when we do see people that are truly humble we see them as weak and ineffective when in truth they have their priorities in order and their focus on what they consider success is unfailing. Our society has placed a ridiculous level of importance on winning and getting instant gratification in all that we do. Placing these expectations in the right trash can is difficult especially for the young people...peer pressure is often a crushing weight that our teens cannot deal with let alone supposedly full grown adults! Humility means that you are very clear on what is important and your place in any success that comes your way…others invested in you to make you successful, your parents, teacher, coaches…somebody other than you is mostly responsible for any success you have…period! Put in the right perspective humility is the natural result, lack of humility comes from a belief that you control more than you really do and can influence outcomes without assistance from others…that's pretty much the antithesis of humility from my perspective.

Early in life I was, and I think we are all very humble in nature. Somewhere along the line that characteristic is replaced with a bombastic nature or at least it was in my case. I was always "the best" at whatever I tried or did…or at least that is what I would tell everyone and that is how I acted. I was never "the best" at anything I did! I was not the best husband and most certainly not the best father and at no time was I a good friend to anybody. Was I adequate at what I did for a profession, yes, because I always moved into more responsible positions but most of the time it was at someone else's expense. I have come to understand that this viewpoint is how entire nations can justify the oppression and or elimination of a people…its easy, just convince yourself that at our most basic core we are better than those we look down on and then it is not that hard to stop looking at them as people with the same feelings and dreams as we do. If we can truly embrace the It's Not About Me concepts then we can get to a much better place, at least personally. Maybe it's way too much to expect us to come together as a nation around this principal because we are so diverse in thoughts, values and actions…one person and one situation at a time though is still a very powerful methodology.

6 EMOTIONAL INVESTMENT

This is a concept that has plagued me for years! To emotionally invest in others outside of your immediate family is what is necessary to develop others to achieve greater results for themselves and the organization(s) that they represent. It is also a conduit of uncertainty, disappointment and most likely pain...or that is how I viewed this for most of my adult life. If I kept people at arm's length then I would not get hurt when they inevitably failed, I would also not be responsible and thus my career path would be safe...in my mind. I am sure that there are entire books written on this subject but when I put this concept into practice I have found it to be singularly rewarding in that I get to know those around me much better and I can have much more in depth conversations about what is important to them and how to design a path that allows them to realize those desires. It has also allowed me to see where there is a complete misalignment between a person's desires and goals and the organization that I represent. This gives me the ability to have those difficult conversations that typically end with a separation between the organization and the individual due to this lack of alignment without significant obstacles.

Emotionally investing in others is exactly what I expect my employer to do with me, even before I was "Enlightened". I would continually ask or complain to my wife about how I was not valued or not listened to and why could they not see just how important I was and my viewpoints were? To my wife's credit her response was that if I was so dissatisfied why did I not pursue a different path of employment? The real answer was that I was more comfortable complaining and blaming others for my misery and if I changed this I would have to take ownership of my own happiness...how crazy is that? To emotionally invest in someone that you work with means that you have to have a heart that truly cares for others...not that we say it, it has to be that we demonstrate this characteristic every day we are interacting. In a very stressful environment are you or can you be that "beacon of hope and inspiration"? Is this something that you value in others around you and a characteristic that readily draws you into a person's sphere of influence? I personally am challenged with this aspect of leadership as I have made myself a typically pessimistic person...how am I addressing this...one day at a time and one situation at a time!

7 TRAINING VERSUS DEVELOPMENT

Understanding the difference between what constitutes training and development is another issue that can get a leader distracted. From my perspective training is in regards to skill sets and or concepts that can be learned and implemented in the everyday aspect of a person's work life. For instance understanding how to lay out a gap analysis is a mathematical exercise that one can learn through training and repetition. Applying the gap analysis concept and process in a live example is part of this training during which we would ask the associate to draw conclusions based upon the data. Development comes from communicating the concept to a client in a way that allows them to see their business through a different set of eyes. This last part is where many people struggle as they are applying the concept in their opinion correctly and they fail to look at the data and conclusions through the clients eyes so there is empathy to the needs of the client and their organization. The effort must be focused on them understanding the concepts and being able to apply them appropriately, their conclusions and actions to take from that may differ from you but again you have to understand what is driving them rather than telling them that their conclusions are wrong and that they should be looking at the outcome differently. Development has a tendency to be very personal in nature because typically a person comes to you for feedback to get better. Feedback comes in many forms but the developmental feedback that assists all of us is typically less than flattering in nature. First of all, if you are the one providing the feedback you have to check you motives for delivering the feedback. Is it to assist the person to get better or make a decision with a better viewpoint or is the feedback being given to drive home something that you find to be very important? Again this activity cannot be about you, it has to be about helping the one receiving the feedback to make the necessary course corrections to assist them in achieving their goals and aspirations. Kept in perspective both Training and Development play an important role in every person's ability to be happy and productive in their lives

8 COURAGE

Many definitions exist for courage, many refer to physical courage such as Rick Rescorla's story. I refer to the courage to stand up for ones convictions regardless of the potential for criticism or being ostracized from a community or group. I guess one could refer to this as moral courage to do what is right or what you believe to be right regardless of the pressure brought to bear on you to conform. In a leadership position you are measured against this every day by those around you, not so much in really what you believe but are you consistent in these beliefs and do you "walk the talk". We have all seen or continue to see people in leadership positions that are critically weak in this area, it is interesting to me that these people do not seem to share any common ground. Some come from the academic world, others the business arena, others in the military. What drives a person to not exhibit the courage needed to follow through with a process to achieve the appropriate outcome...I can only say that this is a fault at the very core of the leader involved, can this be addressed and "fixed"?? As I have and continue to have the same fault in my character, at times, this is something that for me personally is a daily reminder and I am accountable to those around me to measure up to expectations.

A question that I continually ask myself is this "Am I Courageous Leader?" I have had to really think through what that means to me, in my past I defined this by being a tough disciplinarian and brooking no excuses for any lack of success. In my home life it meant that I closed myself off emotionally...to everyone around me. I became an "absent" parent and husband, I allowed...no I expected my wife to be the parent to our boys I played a small role while putting her in the difficult position of trying to provide the discipline and the praise. I am especially embarrassed by these actions with my family, how can a father and husband do these things? At work I was much worse, again I can provide names to call to get others perspectives of my "leadership" style...or lack thereof. Again at 53 years of age I have been shown a different version of what Courage looks, feels and tastes like. Truly learning how to embrace and demonstrate the thought process of *"It's Not About Me"* has been a three year journey that started when I reached out to our CEO of Dewolff, Boberg & Associates for what I thought then was "mentoring".

Actually I was very displeased with how I felt I had been treated by the organization and was, in my mind, giving him the opportunity to "Re-Recruit" me. Basically it was all about me...again! Our CEO, took the time to meet with me while on a project to really get to know me. I was quite impressed by this, then we implemented weekly calls where he called me each Thursday. Due to our Road Warrior lifestyle these calls were at times that were not scripted. He never...never, ever failed to call me on each Thursday and I did test his resolve, again because it was all about me. These conversations began to shift in nature as I actually became more mature in my outlook, I saw in our CEO someone that had significantly changed his outlook on business and life in general. I was deeply moved by this...not easy for me to admit that I saw in him what I was devoid of...humanity! He was deeply committed not just to the organization, he was 110% committed to the people that made up our company. He was willing to invest his time and energy into us...the staff and leaders of DB&A, imagine that a CEO would be willing to spend time with those that were at least three to four levels below his normal sphere of influence. During these conversations he was able to impress upon me his true vision for our company and for him personally in how he viewed or defined success. It wasn't necessarily in financial terms although he is responsible to the board of directors and the shareholders to increase profitability, his vision was one of developing an organization that was being led by servant leaders of the best nature. He saw that through this journey we could not only grow the business but create a company or organization that was not only financially successful but a great place for people to work an entire career. Our CEO embodies what I would call a Courageous Leader and I am so very fortunate and blessed to work with a man of his nature, through his efforts I have begun to embrace the understanding that as a leader it's not about me anymore, my rewards and self-worth come from the growth and success of others...this has been truly powerful in my life!!

9 EMPATHY

My view of Empathy is not one of being able to walk a mile in another's shoes but in getting the individual realigned that they are ready to walk another mile. In order for this to be natural to you as a leader one must understand themselves, implicitly, in order to remain open to new ideas, and concepts. Understanding how you value others is key in truly staying humble in your approach to others that may be struggling. Empathy, in the final accounting, is a worth indicator...what are you willing to invest of yourself to maintain an even viewpoint of yourself? Ultimately this will be indicative of how you are viewed as a leader by those around you.

One of the most powerful events in my life was the birth of our first son, Andrew. When I first held that little bundle I was struck...no dumbfounded by the overwhelming feeling of responsibility holding this little one had on me! I knew that I was responsible for his well-being for all time which meant that I was also on the hook for taking care of his mother...it hit me like a ton of bricks, literally. I was working a third shift at a manufacturing plant located in Everett Washington and before I would leave for work I would take Andrew and rock him to sleep...many times I would actually cry while sitting there with him as the responsibility was crushing...but at no time would I let others see something in me that I had deemed a weakness. Thus began my journey into the black hole of denial and skepticism which wasted entire decades of my life!

When our second son was born and then our third son I was very adept at disguising my true feelings with much bravado and work related items. I worked pretty much seven days a week saying that it was to provide a better life for my family, when in reality I was running away from dealing with my inability to really connect with my wife and kids. I had served my nation in the armed forces, seen combat under deplorable conditions, survived...no thrived in those environments. As a young warrior it was ridiculously easy for me to make the decision that my life was forfeit and thus the stresses and strains of killing or being killed were easy for me to accept. Now I had a family to consider and this did not fit into my mindset of being a young gun! Looking back on my life then I cringe at what I did and said to my wife and family. My father told me many years before that "Youth was wasted on the young" now I know exactly what he meant!

What I see today are young men that are so much better balanced in their outlook on life than I was, each young man that I see go through the birth of their first child demonstrates the same emotions that I had all those years ago. The difference is that they show these emotions much better than I ever could have, I have been afforded the ability to be working with some of these young men and I have been greatly blessed to have had a very small impact on their lives. I cannot wait for my children to have their own! I want to give them the benefit of what mistakes I made if they will hear me. Helping them grow into the awesome dad's and husbands that I know is within them is what keeps my heart beating...also the fact that my wife has expressed her desire that I continue to exist because she has kind of gotten used to having me around. It's not about us...it's about those people at home, our spouses and children are the reason we get up each morning and do what we do, if this is not true in your life then I truly feel sorry for you. Figuring out how to get to this point has taken me over half of my life...please do not waste any more of your time, get your heart right with your spouse and your children. Love openly and with all of your heart and being, make yourself vulnerable in your interactions with those around you...my experience is that you will be impressed with the responses you will receive. Some may not accept the change that you are exhibiting but understand it is because they are being convicted of their superficial lifestyle through your willingness to change!! Stay the course...never, never, ever give up on those around you because the overwhelming feeling of peace and contentment is worth the journey!!

10 OPTIMISM AND CONFIDENCE

A significant part of this is to have received the proper training and development to be viewed as competent in the role of leader. However demonstrating confidence and optimism in the face of most assuredly receiving emotional pain let alone physical pain is something that cannot be assigned as a function of leadership. It must come from deep inside a person, from a place that most of us never really explore or experience. It's easy to show optimism or confidence when the consequences are not necessarily going to be devastating. What about when your own personal livelihood is on the line? Or your physical security is being threatened? Morals, ethics and such are great to have but are meaningless if you are not, as a leader, willing to stand up for those values not matter what. Putting others first means just that...always putting others first in all situations. One basic function of leadership I learned as a new Second Lieutenant in the Army was this...Leaders Eat last!! Always, always, always.

This concept was put to me very plainly but my grizzled old First Sergeant..."While on post sir we salute you as a sign of respect, in a training exercise this is paid back by you putting the men first, in combat this is paid for by standing up when the bullets are flying and saying "follow me" and being the first into harms' way". That was a very eye opening conversation for me as I had never really thought it through in that way. While it's different in business the concept is still valid...Leaders Eat Last!

11 CREDIBILITY

Credibility is something that is earned by a leader, or given by a subordinate. It is something that is earned every day! One misstep and that credibility is destroyed and must be rebuilt with those around you. If this is something that you have to think about then your heart is not really right with the overall concept of "It's Not About You". Developing credibility has to be second nature to a person in a leadership position, if this is forced or if you feel you have to measure this then you should not be in the position. People have the right to be led by those that are technically and tactically proficient, they also have the right to demand that their leaders are accountable and credible in their actions, thoughts and communications. Putting your people first will drive these naturally, without this understanding a leader will struggle and fail over and over because their heart is not aligned with the needs of their people...remember this "Mission First...Men Always" this was the motto used by Army Leadership for many years and it still rings true today.

12 TENACITY AND COMMITMENT

Never, never, ever give up!! Especially on your people, complete commitment to the development of your staff means that your tenacity in pursuing excellence is never ending. Through demonstrating this in a supportive and caring manner your staff will hold themselves to higher standards, they will achieve things that you never believed possible. Again this is something that can be easily corrupted into setting unreasonable expectations of your staff to achieve goals and objectives without the right support from leadership. Doing this destroys everything we have discussed thus far. If there is one thing that my father demonstrated to me many times is that you never give up or give in...ever, there is always something that can be done another approach that can be designed, always. He impressed this upon me so many times that it became second nature to me and I can honestly say that I have never in my life quit anything, no matter what. Giving all you have of yourself is something that our society does not embrace, you give a small portion and then see how that is received and then give a little more depending on what was in it for you. As a leader giving everything you have has to be the minimum expectations...not that we will achieve this but we will always strive for this, when we give with no conditions or boundaries to assist those around us to achieve their goals the rewards are, at least to me, hard to comprehend. Seeing some of those around me raise up and take on seemingly impossible tasks...and succeed is beyond inspirational. I am able to see and experience daily what it is to truly understand and practice the concept of Its Not About Me.

As I have aged, especially over the past three years, this tenet of leadership has taken on a different aspect for me. Tenacity and commitment are now what I owe my family...my family at home and my work family. The complexion of this has taken on a different context at this point in my life, I want to influence more people, positively, than ever before, and due to this I have to look at my health in a different light. I have always been able to count on my body to cash checks that have been increasingly unreasonable. Of late this has been brought home to me in the form of health problems that have robbed me of the physical strength that I have always been able to fall back on in times of stress. I owe a healthy lifestyle to my wife and children in order to be around and part of their lives as long as the good lord allows me to, I also owe this to my work family as I have the correct outlook on life and my heart is right to influence others to take on a more active leadership role regarding understanding it's not about us as leaders. I can never, ever, ever give up on those around me! This is what gets me going each and every day, I truly love what I do and the people I work with. Yes, people are frustrating at times but they are remarkable if you allow them to be! Looking past the frustration or the labels that society puts on people shows us the true person beneath all of that...this has been very difficult for me as I have always been a very judgmental person.

I make snap judgements on a person's inherent worth or lack thereof, then I would not allow that person to change that viewpoint...no matter what. Working through this has been hard for me, I had to work on getting my heart right, my priorities have to continue to evolve to those that are centered around other's needs. I fight this struggle each and every day, it does not come naturally to me I have to get up each day and say to myself that I will do my best to look at things through other people's eyes, to take their feeling into account before speaking...that I will not be HARMFUL to anybody, even strangers that I run across that I may get irritated with. Tenacity and commitment to these goals has challenged me to my very core! But I will never, ever, ever give up...as these are the right things for me to do in my mind.

13 TAKING CARE OF THE "YOU"

I have been talking about putting those around you first in everything you do and think...how does a leader, husband and father feed themselves to remain true to this vision? There are many schools of thought regarding this, all I can do is look at what I am currently working on:

1. <u>Get your priorities right</u>...aka get your heart right. If your thoughts are focused on others your actions will follow and they will become part of who you are going forward.

2. <u>Hold onto your spouse with all of your being!</u> There is a reason that you chose each other, whether it was a year ago or fifty years ago. When you question the validity of the marriage you are questioning the very thing that you are trying to focus on. Too much of our society is telling us to focus on what we want and that we are owed these things whether we have earned them or not. No, a marriage is not an easy thing to work through. Compromise is the key to making the relationship work...from both sides of that equation. My wife and I have been married for thirty years and we plan on another thirty years at least. No it has not always been blissful!! I own most of that discord as everything had to be about me, my wife and I decided when our first child was born that we would buck the trends and she would stay home with the kids. This put significant strain on our meager income at the time and we all know how stressful finances or the lack thereof are on a relationship. We had to save change for a month to take our son to McDonalds for a Happy Meal...Mom and Dad did not have anything but we got much enjoyment from watching him enjoy that hamburger! In a way I miss those days...a much simpler life in many ways.

3. <u>Love openly and often!</u> This is something that I still struggle with daily and most likely will continue to struggle with, that's just me being me and I am a product of my upbringing. Loving my spouse and my children is not difficult...truly loving those I work with is more difficult because it's not something that is typically embraced in corporate America. What I can say is that the organization that I work within has opened itself to me...in essence I know that they love me. Not just for what I bring to the organization but for

me...this is an incredible feeling! How many people can say that they love their job and their employer demonstrates caring and support no matter what the circumstances! This has been a function of the leadership at Dewolff, Boberg and Associates...as a Management Consulting firm when I joined in 2002 this was most definitely not the culture, it was truly a shark tank and only the strongest survived and the most ruthless thrived. Changing that culture to one of nurturing and support has been the work of our CEO...period!

4. <u>Show that you are human</u> As a Project Manager and leader within our company I spent many years NOT showing anybody that I was capable of making a mistake. I blamed others and destroyed lives and careers to make myself look better...I am deeply ashamed of these actions and must take responsibility for them as they were not focused around making anybody better but my situation at the time. Being human was demonstrated to me under some very odd circumstances, or at least I found it odd. I had been promoted to a Chief Of Operations in 2009 and had been operating at this level for three years...not effectively but functionally. I was sat down just before our annual meeting in December of 2011 and told that I was not effective as a Chief and needed to move back to being a Project Manager. I was told this by our Vice President of Operations and during this conversation, which for obvious reasons, I did not take very well it became very evident to me that he was struggling with the conversation. It was a conversation that he did not want to have but had come to the realization or had been brought the realization that this course of actions was the correct one not only for the company but me personally as well. In this moment I saw him not as a "boss" but as a person and although the transition was difficult and painful it has been the best thing that happened to me in my professional life. Seeing the obvious struggle that he was having with the conversation showed me that he cared...I did not really appreciate the caring at the time but as with most things those that do not kill you make you stronger. Care enough about your people to tell them when they are not achieving expectations, as leaders we owe them this communication. We also owe them the support and time to make the changes necessary to overcome the things that they are struggling with. But how can any of us get "better" if we are not made aware of the things that we are falling short on? Giving well

deserved praise is wonderful and everyone is happy to do this, in the same vein giving well deserved feedback to our people needs to be viewed in the same light. If we never have to confront poor behavior or results that are not acceptable how does an organization continue to grow? Identifying the gap between the desired performance levels and the current levels is how we assist organizations and people to achieve greater successes, without this there is no need to strive for better things.

5. Set High Expectations for yourself and for those around you. Setting expectations that are easily achieved do not help people or organizations become world class! If you truly invest yourself in your people and your organization you will achieve results that are just unbelievable and you will find that those that may report directly to you are capable, many times, of better planning, better strategy development, better products etc... As a leader learn to get out of the way! Let your people be the people they can be, support them, led them, inspire them...but get the hell out of their way!

14. BE QUIET AND LISTEN

This tenant of leadership has meant different things to me over the years. First, during my younger life it was a very mechanical thought process in which I felt this meant that I should sit quietly and listen to others. I would do this but I never really listened to what others were saying, I was always thinking about my response to their points and how I would prove to them and to others why my point view was right...always. I would take over conversations with my viewpoints and shut down any and all other points of view, because wasn't this supposed to be all about me and how great I am...how did the others not understand that?

During a specific time in my military career I was introduced to a very different take on this. I was taught to walk point in hostile territory by a man that was a full blooded native American, his tribe really doesn't matter, but what he taught me was or could have been life changing. I learned some basics into spotting things that may have been out of place and some rudimentary tracking techniques but what was the hardest for me to understand was what was termed "being still" obviously I thought he meant standing or lying still, no what he meant was quieting my intellect and my emotions to allow my spirit to become in tune with my surroundings. I know that this sounds like a new age thought process but it was very effective in allowing me to open my mind to input that I would normally have dismissed. This allowed me to determine that I was going left instead of right, that I would take them over the hill not around it...without really knowing why these decisions were impressed upon me as surely as if someone was standing next to me whispering in my ear. When I followed this process I was successful in avoiding dangerous situations, when I used my intellect and my emotions I caused the team to get involved in actions that would ultimately get people killed. When I left the military I mentally compartmented these experiences and drove them from my thoughts. I never really considered that these skills could be used in the business or corporate world.

Based upon my recent past I have resurrected this process and I am in the process of applying it to what I do as a leader within the company I work for and in my personal life as well. I had to change how I listened to people, either people I worked with or my family. I would not just listen to the words they spoke but pay close attention to how they said it. I look at their eyes, their body language, their tone of voice when they say certain things because I have found that in many instances the person talking is trying to ascertain what it is that you are looking for and their words are designed to give you the feeling that you and they are aligned in your thoughts when in reality you could not be further apart. When I sense that the words and the mannerisms do not match up I will typically ask the question "Is what we are talking about what you really wanted to talk to me about or is there something else? Because I am sensing that there is another topic you would like to discuss?" Almost 100% of the time when I do this the person I am in conversation with will sit back in their chair or step back and take a moment to assess if you are being honest in wanting them to open up or if you are a potential threat to them. About 50% of the time I am successful in getting them to really discuss what they need to discuss, the failure rate that I am seeing is strictly due to my inability to communicate more effectively.

I said that in the past I tried to dominate conversations because it had to be about me, I find that now I tend to do the same thing but for different reasons! I have such tremendous passion for the experiences that I have undergone and I have received such incredible support both at home and with my work family that I want everyone to understand it. I am coming to the conclusion that my ability to influence others is directly tied to how I demonstrate, each and every day, my commitment to this lifestyle of putting others first. Based upon the type of person I have been...mean, nasty, ego centric etc... many do not believe that a person like that can truly change and you know they may be right because I cannot say that I do not have my selfish and ego centric moments. What I can say is that when these occur I have to go back to a basic premise that I use which is that "I Will Do No Harm" I get up each morning, look at myself in the mirror (yes that is scary) and tell my refection that I will do no harm today. Every day I am sure that I fail at this but my motivations come from a different place now, I have come to grips with my mortality and have an intense desire to influence and impact others positively be they members of my family or members of my work family.

People will have the need to label this or categorize this as a "Religious" or "New Age" thought process...I truly do not care about the labels I just want as many people to experience what I have experienced and share in the peace that comes with this different level of conciseness that has been afforded me. Finding a way to "Be Quiet And Listen" is going to be very personal...for me I like to listen to what I find to be motivational music. It can be any type or genre of music I am looking for something that speaks to my soul and allows me to calm my intellect and emotions to truly open myself up to suggestions as to how I can become better...a better father, husband or leader. Again this is specific to me and each person will find their own way if they want to...I strongly endorse finding a way to quiet your intellect in order to open yourself up to greater thoughts and actions.

15. Caring Unconditionally

Helping or being helpful takes many different forms and these concepts tend to change depending upon your perspective. Early in my children's life "helping" to me meant that I provided for my family mostly from a financial aspect, I was not really motivated to be there or "help" from an emotional point of view. I felt I was a good dad, I played with my children all the time, I made time to read to them, put them to bed, give them bath's etc... but did I really demonstrate my unconditional love? Unconditional love...now there is a term that has terrified me for most of my adult years! When I was a child I was like every other child, I wanted to make my parents happy or proud of me and you know I think that this was achieved for the most part. My father was not one given to showing his emotions most of the time, but it was the little things that he would do that showed me how much he cared about me. As I have gotten older the act of "Unconditional Love" has taken on a different meaning. I am my father's son...and due to that I pretty much have followed in his footsteps regarding displaying emotion. As I have reflected back upon my life and began to really understand the experiences that I have been afforded, the family both personal and work that I have been so blessed with I have begun to understand that people, whether these people be my children, my wife, my co-workers, my neighbor's etc... they all have the same desire for people to show them caring...unconditionally.

In my personal life I have begun to try to enact this principal with my children, my wife and my son's wives. I am finding that I am singularly horrible at demonstrating this type of love or caring. I am so tremendously proud of my son's and the type of people they have grown up to be that my chest almost bursts...as do all Mom's and Dad's. Why can't I just tell them how much they mean to me? Why do I think that it will sound weird coming from me and that they will think that this old man has lost his mind...most likely they would absolutely love hearing those comments from me, I will achieve this even if it kills me!! With my wife this has become much easier over the thirty years we have been married. As we have grown old together I cannot help but remember the saying that refers to that behind every man is a greater woman...my wife has never been "behind" me in anything that we have done, she has been side by side with me or she has been leading our family. She has demonstrated unconditional love to me many times due to my trying her patience and downright testing her faith. To not cherish this woman would be a sin of enormous magnitude! I have most definitely not demonstrated the same level of unconditional love and caring to her over these thirty years and I am working hard to make up for that lost time.

In my professional life this has also been undergoing significant changes. Early on in my career I felt that demonstrating caring for others that I worked with was tantamount to showing weakness and that this must be avoided at all costs. I felt that in order to be an effective leader I had to treat everybody the same...like a dog. When I joined the current company that I work for this was the culture that I stepped into so I fit into this very easily. In this management consulting firm it was the quintessential shark tank...those with the biggest teeth and dorsal fins were the ones that succeeded. This meant that you destroyed those around you that had any weakness at any time! Ruthlessness was a trait that was promoted and held in high regard by the leaders that I observed. As I said I fit into this like a glove...I was very successful because I had no issues with treating those around me as less than human, what I wanted was more important than other peoples thoughts. My desires were put to the forefront rather than addressing other's needs, I fed my ego all the time. Terminating people was viewed by the company as a badge of honor, the more you terminated the higher regard for you there was! Hopefully I have painted a very dysfunctional picture here as that is exactly what it was...dysfunctional, only the few were rewarded while the many did all the work and suffered all of the horrible treatment, sound familiar to anybody? As I said earlier in this it was around 2012 that a significant change began to occur at this dysfunctional company. Our CEO was making a concerted effort to change the outlook of the leadership, starting at the very top of the organization. As we are in the business of change management and continuous improvement we all understood the very essence of what it takes to change an organization from the inside out...we just never looked at our organization the same way and here our CEO was applying the same concepts to us! We reacted exactly the same way that all of our clients typically react, or at least I did. Absolutely we needed to change...change that other guy first because I am good! That is exactly what I thought, that I did not need to get any "better" but the others needed to get on the same page as me because I was the best...wasn't I? It took about two years for the reality to sink into me and by sink in I really mean that I was convicted by my exposure to a different style of leadership...and it hurt, deeply. I always knew that what I was doing was wrong and hurtful but I thought that this was the only way for me to "get mine".

I have stated earlier that I reached out to my CEO for mentoring but what I was really doing was giving him the chance to re-recruit me as I was in the process of leaving the company because I was convinced that they had no idea nor did they really care about me. When I reached out to him he took the time to get to know me, I mean really get to know me. Then he set up the expectation that he would call me each and every Thursday...did you read that...HE WOULD CALL ME, not the other way around. He called me every week on Thursday when he had time to an hour conversation with me. As these conversations progressed I began to understand that he had undergone significant changes in his viewpoints and priorities...our people were more important than those that were in leadership positions...It wasn't about him anymore it was about everybody else. How did I miss this significant transformation? Because I was being very selfish and because of that I transmitted this to others that they had to feel the same way...didn't they? I began to see the vision that he had for the company and I was completely bought into it!! I bought into it because I knew that this was the right thing and that we were on a trajectory to become a company that one could spend an entire working lifetime with and be proud of the body of work that you were involved with. He stuck with our conversations no matter what, he invested in me unconditionally and that is the model that I have been convicted with...now it is about how do I pay this forward?

16. PAY IT FORWARD

Paying it forward...that was the name of a great movie and in that movie the concept was very clearly communicated. We all know that we should pay the kindness of others forward to those we encounter throughout our lives...but we don't always do that, why is that? All I can do is talk about this from my perspective as I cannot talk for everybody. Let me try to give you an example of how I do not "Pay It Forward", my profession requires me to travel pretty much 100% of the time, I fly at least twice per week sometimes more. On an average year I spend 48 weeks a year in a hotel so my working lifestyle is of a "Road Warrior" mentality. From this lifestyle I have developed an intense dislike for airports and everything about them. Initially I took this out on the TSA representatives and was afforded the opportunity of seeing the inside of many detention rooms at different airports across the country. Once I figured out that this was just inconveniencing me I switched that intense dislike to the people that were in the airport...all of these people that would just meander across my path would send me into a rage. When I boarded the plane I did not want to talk with anybody and I mean anybody, if you had the unfortunate distinction of sitting beside me during this time of my life I truly apologize for being such a jerk.

On many occasions I had seatmates that were very nice and personable, they tried to establish a conversation with me and I was so self-absorbed that I would just shut them out...rudely. Once I was able to view this with a different heart I saw those people for what they were...Angels sent to me to give me a modicum of peace in a chaotic environment. So recently I tried this out myself, I was sitting down on a flight from Atlanta GA to Los Angeles CA. I was on the aisle seat like I normally am and this lady was sitting next to me, she came up and indicated that she was sitting next to me and then attempted to lift the heavy roller bag she had to place it in the overhead. I stood up and asked her if I might be able to help her with that bag and she accepted, then when we were both sitting down and she was all situated I leaned over and asked her if she was having a good day or if she was struggling. She looked at me initially like I was crazy but I continued on about how I really did not like the traveling experience and how ridiculous was it for me to continue to do what I do. She leaned back in her seat and took out her knitting needles and asked me how crazy was it for her to be able to go through security with these sharp implements...we both were able to have a good laugh about that. This trip turned out to be a very enjoyable one and the time passed quickly due to both of us making an effort to enjoy each other's company.

In my professional life I have received many gifts from those that have taken the time to invest in my development. Until now I have most definitely not "Paid It Forward" I looked at these investments as "owed" to me as wasn't everything about me? Due to my acceptance and conviction regarding that leadership means that nothing is about me anymore I am looking for ways to assist others in achieving success as they define it not me. What I am finding is that even though my heart is right and my motives are clean I still get in my own way when trying to do this. I still do not communicate clearly to others that are asking or in need of being invested in and due to this I fail continually at being that motivating influence that I desire to be. I have come to the conclusion that one cannot undo in a few months what you have built up over an entire lifetime...even if you have achieved a significant change of heart. This is also a process and as with all things that are process related it takes repetition and perseverance to achieve any lasting results. So I work at this each and every day, one person at a time and one conversation at a time...that is how I am "Paying It Forward".

17. LEADERS INFLUENCE OUTCOMES

The more I talk and interact with people the more I find that the most important tenant of leadership is influencing others. Most of you may be saying...Really it's taken you this long to see this? Perhaps we are seeing things a bit differently though. Influencing others to do what you want them to do for the benefit that you want either for yourself or for the organization that you are working for is, to me, selfish in nature. Influencing others to take actions, change behaviors, or change their focus for the good of them both personally and professionally, again to me, epitomizes the concept of It's Not About Me!

Whether we acknowledge it or not when we move into a leadership position be that as a parent or within our companies we begin to look for ways to influence others here are some of the types that I have identified over the years.

1. <u>Best Buddy</u> – This type of leader feels that if he or she is friendly with those around them that these people will feel inclined to do what they are asking because we are "Best Buddies". When these same people do not see things the way they want them to they feel betrayed because...look at all I have done for you, how can you not do what I want? These types of behaviors will quickly lead to a significant "Victim" mentality where they see themselves as being victimized by those around them and this leads to the downward spiral.

2. <u>Captain Of The Ship</u> – This type of leadership style is one that isolates those in a leadership position from those around them. As the "Captain Of The Ship" I will not allow myself to become emotionally invested in anyone that I am around, either at work or at home. If I take this action then I cannot be hurt by those around me because I know that I will be hurt because it has happened before and I will not allow that to happen to ME again. Many times this attitude is developed from the "Best Buddy" style when they begin to feel victimized by those around them because they are not getting what they want.

3. <u>Dictator</u> - People in this category have progressed past the "Captain Of The Ship" style and have convinced themselves that they are the very best at whatever it is that they are doing

and therefore you should do what I tell you to do. There is no mentorship, creativity or imagination allowed in this world...there is only my way or the highway! Ring anybody's bell?? This defines my leadership style for many years! People that engage in this type of leadership style have convinced themselves that if everybody would just do what they tell them to do everything would be perfect. Most importantly when people actually do what they tell them to do and things do not work out the way they should then obviously they did not do it right because they "The Dictator" cannot be wrong...right? This is where I existed for much of my time in leadership positions, perhaps there are times where this type of leadership style is needed such as in the military when you are in combat but other than that I struggle with finding a situation in civilian life where this type of oppressive style is called for.

4. Interactive – This is kind of, to me, the culmination of the above types of leadership styles. As I progressed through these I have come to a place where It's Not About Me or what I want anymore...it's all about what those around me need. The clients that work with, my work family and most importantly my wife and children and yes our friends are or have to be more important than what I want. By focusing my efforts on assisting, coaching, mentoring and listening I put myself in a position to become a positive influence in other people's lives and that will or has ultimately led to my fulfillment as a leader, husband and father.

Influencing others in a positive manner, again to me, has a process or I have come to recognize a process that when I follow it the outcomes are very positive and when I don't the outcomes are very bad:

a. *Check My Motivations* – I have to understand why I am having the interaction that I am having...is it to assist the other person or am I irritated at this person for something or another? You do not always have the opportunity to prepare adequately for all interactions but if you can mentally check your motivations you can change the outcome to be a win...win for each of you.

b. _Words Matter_ – Choosing the words that you use when you are trying to influence others is extremely important, I never thought this but this concept was brought to my attention by people around me that have invested in my development over the years. I always felt that if I said something that hurt your feelings then that meant that you were weak minded and I would continue to follow this path because I am "helping" you by trying to reduce your sensitivity to the words being used. If you will read the above sentence again and reflect upon that you can see just how horrible a person and boss I was being!!

c. _Change Perspectives_ – What I mean by this is to change my perspective to that of the person that I am talking with or interacting with. Seems like an easy thing to do right? We are always taught to "put ourselves in the other person's shoes" right? Yet we or rather I very rarely would really do that. I have found that in order for me to do this effectively I have to not only listen to the words that the other person is saying but listen to their tone, watch their eyes and be aware of their body language...putting this all together will allow me to change my perspective because I am investing in them rather than trying to make my point.

d. _Transparency_ – I am speaking about being very open and honest about why you are having the conversation. If I have done the first three things then I am able to communicate clearly and compassionately what it is at risk without making judgements upon the person that I am talking with. I find this part of being able influence others the hardest as it means that I have to communicate to another person what amounts to a value judgement without putting my values first. If I am truly invested in the other person and what they need to progress in whatever we are talking through then I owe this open and honest communication to them...because I truly care.

e. *Feedback* – I am not referring to giving feedback, I am talking about receiving feedback. Again this is not a strength that I readily possess, receiving feedback from those that we are supposed to be leading difficult for most of us I feel. In order for me to receive that type of feedback or any type for that matter I have to remain focused on the concept of it's not about me. Early on in my conversations with our CEO he made it a point to explain the need for people to "empty their buckets". I did not understand this until we talked at length about that everybody carries the "wounds" or "wrongs" that have been done to them over the years. By allowing others to "empty their bucket" with you it enables the two of your to have better conversations regarding the real needs. Having the ability to allow others to empty their buckets means that you have to be able to hear that you may be the reason for the hurt. Being in a position to allow others to empty their buckets with me is something that I am working toward, it takes a significant amount of maturity and selflessness to achieve this, again being able to interact on a weekly basis with a leader that is capable of this level of caring has helped me immensely.

18. LEADERS EAT LAST

I made a brief reference to this tenant under **Optimism and Confidence** and I would like to expound upon this a bit. I experienced this basic leadership tenant after I was commissioned as an Officer in the Army, out on field training exercises our Battalion Commander and Company Commander told us all that as leaders of men we would always put our needs behind those of our men...meaning that we would always eat last. While I was in the Military I adhered to this precept as that is how I was trained...I obviously did not internalize this concept as when I left the military and went into my civilian life I did exactly the opposite!

For many years I looked at things from a very selfish standpoint...why did I have to put others first when I saw at work and around our society that those that put themselves first were getting rewarded while those that were practicing the art of true leadership were getting kicked to the curb...Nice guys finish last right? So I charged off merrily putting myself first, in the beginning I told myself that I was doing this to ensure that my family was getting what I wanted them to get, then, gradually it became all about me in every aspect of my life. It's not like I realized this and did it with full forethought...this happened over time as I became more and more disillusioned with the value system that our society rewarded. I saw that we were becoming more and more focused on the instantaneous gratification rather than working for something, we expected to get what we wanted just because. I talked with my wife and others about this with disdain...all the while I was participating in this destructive behavior. I continue to see this behavior, not just in our young people but in all aspects of our lives...I still go down this path at times myself and have to be continually held accountable to the concept of it can't be about me.

Transformation or rather the embracing of this simple leadership tenant occurred for me through much reflection and interaction with the person that I looked at as my mentor. I knew intellectually that leaders should always put their people or organizations first, I understood conceptually why this was important but I would never take the personal actions necessary to demonstrate this those around me...not even my family! In the many discussions that I have had and continue to have with our CEO this has been impressed upon me over and over again, not through his words but through his actions...the fact that he is joyful in taking his time and talking with me each week has made a huge difference. However this difference would never have taken place without me opening my heart to actually hearing what he was talking with me about. As I listened to him and continued to have our discussions it became more and more evident that many of the things that my wife would try to talk with me about were the same things that my CEO was impressing upon me!! That really forced me to reevaluate my priorities and how I listened and treated my wife...then I had to rethink how I interacted with my family and then, low and behold, I had to completely rethink how I was interacting with my work family. I did this but I was doing it very slowly as I was still holding back because if I really and fully engaged what I knew to be right...how would people view me?

The last part of this was that I got sick, I mean really sick and I could not figure what was going on. I had always been able to call upon my body and stubborn will to overcome any physical ailments, but what I was experiencing I could not will away no matter what I did. We found out that my Gall Bladder was filled with stones and I decided that Ok we found the problem and now we can just get that taken care of and I can get on with my life...like always. In the process to schedule me for the surgery they conducted a cardiogram (EKG) on me and found that I had issues with my heartbeat...it would flutter. I had to undergo the placement of a stent in one of my arteries in my heart before they would take my gall bladder out. I also found out that I had blockages in three main arteries in my heart, one was 40% blocked, one was 90% blocked, and one was 100% blocked. They inserted the stint into the 90% blocked one which helped me quite a bit. However they could not operate on the gall bladder for another four to five weeks...those additional weeks with my gall bladder basically rotting in my body almost killed me...literally. After they got in and removed my gall bladder and I was recovering in the hospital...my wife never left my side...ever!! I came to the understanding that my time left on this earth was limited, I also had to face the fact that I had wasted much of my life by making everything about me. I am deeply ashamed and embarrassed by how I treated everybody...EVERYBODY around me and I wish I could apologize to everyone I have hurt over my 53 years of life. I made the connection between what I had been going through and my mortality and from that connection I decided that I wanted my legacy to be one of positive influence instead of negativity and the deadly and insidious "but" that we are all used to hearing...You did a great job son, **_but_** if you would have just tried harder you would have made a bigger difference. Have you ever heard that from a parent, a coach, an employer?? Have you ever used that word in that way with those around you? I am trying very hard to get that word out of my vocabulary...**_but_** I fail miserably every day, as I continue to grow in understanding that it can't be about me I will succeed at removing this, however it is a battle each day, at least it is for me.

19. ACCOUNTABILITY

For those of you that are sitting back saying...All this is well and good but how do you performance manage those that need it? If all of this seems to be a little to utopian for you, let me try to bring these concepts full circle. If one is truly committed to the leadership concept of it's not about you then giving open and honest feedback to those in need of it in order to influence or create a more positive outcome is part of our responsibility. Giving people feedback that is less than positive is never easy...especially if you truly care about the person, which is why I would always not emotionally invest in those that I was responsible for, if I cared for them then it became much harder to give that feedback...exactly!!

In the line of business that I am in, ensuring that there is good alignment not just with the client group we are working with but with those on a given project team is critical to over delivering results. In order to do that we as leaders have to ensure that we have a team that not only possesses the right skill sets but is behaviorally and attitudinally aligned. Doing this ends up being the primary duty of a leader, not the technical aspects of the job, whatever it is. When a team member is struggling but is putting forth the effort to get better it is very easy, as a leader, to dismiss any errors or omissions because the person is really trying...this is a trap that I have fallen into many times. I have to be cognizant of the person's abilities and ensure that I have set them up for success and are supporting them in their efforts...however if their lack of abilities is impacting the team in how they deliver results then I owe it to the team and the organization to performance manage that person out of the company as they are not a good fit. Doing this for the right reasons is never wrong and typically will lead to the person being separated finding a better fit for them making them much happier...not at the time you have to separate them but in time. By adjusting my attitude and adopting the concepts I have discussed here I find that it is much easier for me to have these conversations with anybody. If I truly care about what is best for them and aligning that with what is best for the team and the company these decisions become much easier...at least it has worked that way for me.

A CONTINUING JOURNEY

I was advised by several people that are much more adept and knowledgeable than I that I needed to make this a much more standard selection, more in tune with other "Self Help" books. Although the advice was meant to help me get a more sellable product to market and it was much appreciated, my purpose for writing this was more cathartic in nature than anything else.

I cannot put an "epilogue" to this work as I am still working through how to live and apply this basic tenant on a daily basis both in my personal life and my professional one as well. As I continue down the path I will, I am sure, want to come back and add to this work in order to capture items, actions or behaviors that are made more evident to me over time. No this piece of work is not "standard" in any way...it is intensely personal and I meant it to be that way as I believe that we all have similar experiences or will have them. From these experiences comes an abundance of life experiences that are typically repressed and viewed as not value added especially in the business world. Based upon my current position in life I must completely disagree with this, making one's self vulnerable is the most terrifying thing that I have ever done or engaged in...it has been also the most fulfilling action I have ever experienced as well. Vulnerability does not equal weakness either mentally or behaviorally, on the contrary, those that make themselves vulnerable in order to focus their efforts on others are some of the very best leaders you can ever come in contact with. If you want to grow, either personally or professionally, becoming more vulnerable will exceed your expectations...or at least that has been my experience.

www.ingramcontent.com/pod-product-compliance
Lightning Source LLC
Chambersburg PA
CBHW072258200526
45168CB00016B/2142

* 9 781517 056131 *